CONTENTS

Ancient Greece

The Ancient Greeks made many discoveries. Some of them, like their medical discoveries, were passed down to us over time. Others, like the use of steam power, we had to discover for ourselves all over again.

Many things that the Greeks discovered were just ideas. Very few of their inventions and discoveries were used. Ideas mattered far more to the Ancient Greeks than putting those ideas to use.

Timeline

First city states 800BC	447BC Parthenon begun	
	War with Persia	Rule of Alexander
776BC First Olympic Games	Salamis 480BC	146BC Romans take over Greece
	Marathon 490BC	

A Greek man and his **slave**. One reason why the Greeks did not make inventions (such as the steam engine) do work for them was because there were plenty of slaves to do the work instead.

ARISTOTLE, A **PHILOSOPHER**, EXPLAINS ANCIENT GREEK THINKING IN ABOUT 350BC:

It is clear that the men who began to think about these things wanted to know things for their own sake, not for any practical use they might make of the knowledge. People did not begin to try to find out about the way things work until they had made themselves comfortable in life. They did it for entertainment.

Ancient Greeks were the first people to think about how people should organize themselves. Greek philosophers wrote about how **city states** should be run. Their most famous system, in which all **citizens** have a say in how their country is run, is called **democracy**. This word comes from a Greek word 'demos' (which means people) and 'kratios' (which means power).

DEMOCRACY IN ACTION IN ATHENS

Whenever there was a decision to be made, every male citizen who wanted a say went along to discuss what to do. Anyone who wanted to speak could do so. Then everyone voted on what to do. They also chose **officials** to make sure that **taxes** were paid, laws were kept, and so on.

DID EVERYONE HAVE A SAY?

Not everyone had a say in Athens, even though it was a democracy. Women, children, **slaves** and people who came from other places could not vote, work as an official or be on a jury.

Decision-making meetings in Athens were held first in the agora, the main public place in the city. A special meeting place, the Pnyx, was later built on a hill outside the town. In this picture of the Pnyx, a decision is being discussed.

Because the Ancient Greeks thought learning was important, they also thought it was important to write everything down. At first they wrote things down by carving stones or writing on wax or clay. Then they used **papyrus** paper from Egypt, either for paper scrolls or books.

PUBLIC LIBRARIES

It was important to collect information together in one place, such as a library, so that people could use it. The Greeks were the first people in the western world to want libraries which could be used by many people, not just a few **priests** or **scholars**.

ALEXANDRIA

The greatest Greek library was set up in Alexandria, in Egypt, in about 290BC. It was set up by an Egyptian pharaoh, although most of the scholars who worked in the library and the nearby university were Greek. They were so keen to get hold of as many valuable documents as they could, they bought them, borrowed them to copy them, and even stole them!

The library of Alexandria

The Ancient Greeks loved stories. They wrote stories about gods and goddesses and how they interfered with the lives of ordinary people. They wrote stories about the past too. They were the first people to write down all these stories, although they sometimes got real events tangled up with imaginary ones.

MYTHS

The Greek myths are famous. They are stories about the Greek gods. Many of these stories are still told today because they are so exciting. They are full of battles and adventures.

HISTORY

One of the earliest stories written by the Greeks is the *Iliad*, written by Homer in about 700BC. The *Iliad* tells the story of Troy, an Ancient Greek city. Some of the story is made up, such as the parts in which gods appear. But many people think some of it is true. **Archaeologists** have found evidence of battles in places mentioned in the stories.

Many Greek vases had pictures on them illustrating famous Greek myths. This picture comes from the story of the travels of a hero called Odysseus. The creatures flying around the boat are Sirens. They are singing beautiful songs to lure the sailors to crash on to the rocks. Odysseus has stuffed his sailors' ears with wax so that they cannot hear the songs. He has tied himself to the mast so that he cannot steer the boat on to the rocks.

The Ancient Greeks wrote many books. They also kept lists of who had paid their **taxes**, who had been to court for committing a crime, who had worked as an **official** and who was a **citizen**. They wrote thousands of official documents.

SECRET MESSAGES

Greek armies had many sneaky ways of sending messages that the enemy could not work out.

• In about 400BC the Spartans sent messages on long strips of paper. They wound each strip around a wooden rod and wrote the message on it, from top to bottom. Then they unwound the paper and filled in the gaps with more letters. If the enemy got hold of the message all they had was a long strip of paper covered in letters. But when the message got to the right person who had a wooden rod like the one used to write the message, they wrapped the strip around it and read the message.

• In about 170BC a soldier called Polybius used a system of burning torches to send messages. The torches were waved to spell out letters of the alphabet. It was so complicated the messages had to be short!

An army encampment. Someone is making a record of stores, another is reading a secret message and someone else is sending a torch message.

The Ancient Greeks seem to have been among the first people to see childhood as a separate stage of life that is different to adulthood. Most earlier peoples seem to have expected children to learn adult ways as soon as possible.

FUN AND GAMES

Greek babies and toddlers grew up playing many games that children play today. They had rattles and dolls. They had toy soldiers and they had board games, like chess and draughts. As they grew up, boys played early forms of rugby and hockey.

When boys were about 13 years old and when girls were married – usually between the ages of 14 and 18, they took their toys to a **temple** and left them as presents for the god or goddess of the temple. They were then grown-ups. Many of their offerings have been found by **archaeologists**.

A **vase painting** of an Ancient Greek child on a potty and a photo of a modern child on an Ancient Greek potty found in Athens.

We give rattles to babies so that, while playing with this, they do not break any of the furniture; for young things cannot keep still!

If a boy is to be a good farmer, or builder, he should play at farming, or at building toy houses, using small tools like the ones that real farmers and builders use.

In Ancient Greece there were two kinds of medicine. One was partly magical. The other used ideas about keeping healthy and examining patients carefully – ideas that doctors still believe in today.

In about 400BC, the Greek doctor Hippocrates wrote down the first rules about how to treat a patient (called the Hippocratic Oath), which doctors still follow today. Many Greek doctors used **herbal cures**. Many of the plants they used are still used as medicines now.

MAGICAL MEDICINE

One of the many Greek gods was Asclepios, the god of medicine. Magical medicine was carried out in **temples** to Asclepios, which were built all over Greece. Patients went to leave a present at the temple and sleep there for at least one night. Asclepios was supposed to visit them and cure them, sometimes giving them a magical dream too. The **priests** of the temple also looked after them, often using herbal cures.

Asclepios is shown treating a patient in a dream in his temple.

This doctor is treating a patient in a clinic. He is taking blood from the patient.

KEEPING HEALTHY

Many doctors believed it was important to keep fit, eat well and exercise. They said this would stop someone from becoming ill. When patients were ill doctors gave them herbal cures, keeping careful notes on how the cures worked. They tried not to operate. They had noticed that people often died after operations, from shock, loss of blood or **infections**.

The Greeks were not the first people to realize that it was important to keep themselves and their towns clean in order to keep healthy. But they were the first people to make sure that there were public **fountains** and bath houses, and that the streets were regularly cleared of rubbish.

CLEAN WATER

Public fountains in Greek towns used pure spring water that had come down from the mountains. People tried not to use water from streams or rivers that might have been **polluted**. The water from public fountains was used for washing clothes and also for all cooking and drinking. People also collected rainwater in huge pottery jars, but it did not rain often enough for this to give them all the water they needed.

These women are getting water from a public fountain.

This is a model of a woman in a bath. Greek baths were not long enough to lie down in.

CLEAN PEOPLE

People were told to wash regularly to keep healthy. Some people with large houses had a washroom at home with a large pottery bowl on a stand to wash from. Some cities also had public baths. These had warm rooms and hot water. They had baths and at least some of them had showers, too. Some people thought it was weak to go to baths and not wash at home in cold water!

ADVICE ABOUT STAYING HEALTHY, WRITTEN BY A DOCTOR IN ABOUT 350BC:

Every day, after rising, a man should rub his body with oil. Then he should wash his hands and face with pure water. He should rub his teeth inside and out with peppermint powder, to clean them. He should clean his nose and ears with oil.

It does not rain much in Greece so fresh water is precious. The thinker and inventor, Archimedes, worked out a way to lift water from the river so that it could be used to water plants. This system is still used to lift water out of the River Nile in Egypt today.

THE FIRST FIRE ENGINE

Many Greek inventions were never used. But fire engines were because, if they got to the fire fast enough, they were much more efficient than people passing buckets of water.

The first fire engine was designed in about 250BC. It was improved by Heron of Alexandria so that the water could be squirted in any direction. Heron lived in the Greek **colony** of Alexandria, in Egypt, where many **philosophers** and inventors settled to use the big library there. Heron's fire engine was used right through Roman times. **Archaeologists** have found the remains of a fire engine in the Roman remains of Silchester, England. It would have been in use in about AD350.

A fire engine in action.

MAPS

The Greeks knew that the world was round. In about 290BC the thinker Eratosthenes said it was 40,000 kilometres round. He was only 67 kilometres out! They worked out the lines of **latitude** and **longitude**, which we still use on our maps today.

SKY MAPS

Heracleides drew a map of the planets, putting them in their correct order from the Earth. He worked out how far away they were too. His only error was to say that the Sun went around the Earth.

MEASURING TIME

The Greeks used water clocks where water ran from one pottery jar into another. Athens had a large, town water clock. It had a float inside, joined to a marker outside. This pointed to marks on the outside of the jar that showed the time. Later water clocks were very complicated. One, made in about 270BC, used the moving water to ring bells, move small dolls and even make birds sing.

A mosaic picture of Anaximander. He made a map of the world and also invented a sundial to tell the time.

PYTHAGORAS

The Greek thinker Plato said 'God is always doing **geometry**'. The Ancient Greeks certainly were. One of the most famous mathematical thinkers is Pythagoras, who worked out many of the ideas in maths that we still use. When you work with shapes and angles, do long division or even more complicated algebra. you are using ideas passed down from the Greeks.

Modern school children still use Pythagoras' mathematical ideas.

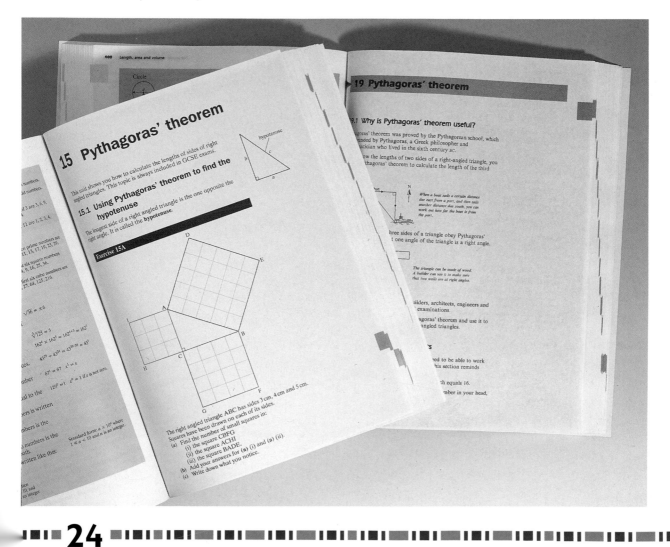

THE FIRST COMPUTER?

In about 1900 a Greek ship that had been wrecked was found. It held bronze and marble statues and a pile of cogs and gears, all with writing on. Some people thought they were part of a machine to work out directions. Other people thought they were part of a machine to show how the planets moved. In 1971, after twenty years of working on the puzzle, a university professor found out the answer. It was a complicated machine for working out the date many years ahead – a very early, simple computer.

Ancient Greek ideas about maths and about how to behave were passed down to us in books. But other ideas were lost, either because they were not written down or because the books did not survive. Some writers from the time said things in passing that suggest the Greeks understood the ideas behind jet engines and steam power.

GADGETS

Greek thinkers used many of their ideas to make clever gadgets and toys. They made mechanical toy theatres and magical inkpots that never spilled ink, no matter how you turned them. They thought clever people should not bother to make useful things.

There are some exceptions. Heron of Alexandria used steam power to open heavy brass **temple** doors – this made the temple more magical and mysterious. The Ancient Greeks also made fighting machines, including an early machine-gun that fired a row of arrows.

Mines, like the ones that these **slaves** are working in, could
have been easier to work in with steam engines to pump out
the water. The Greeks had steam power but they did not see
why they needed to make slaves comfortable.

EVIDENCE FROM THE TIME

We know what the Ancient Greeks knew from books that were written at the time. These books were copied out and passed down. But many books may have been lost, so the Greeks may have understood many more things — we shall never know for sure.

A Greek carving which shows the words and music of an early Greek song of praise to the god Apollo. **Archaeologists** have worked out what this would have sounded like.

SOMETIMES GREEK WRITERS SAY THINGS WHICH GIVE US CLUES THAT THEY KNEW ABOUT THINGS THAT WE HAVE NO EVIDENCE FOR. WHILE WRITING ABOUT ELEPHANTS, ARISTOTLE ACCIDENTALLY TELLS US ABOUT AN INVENTION FOR DIVERS:

Divers are given breathing instruments, so they can draw air from above the water, which lets them stay underwater for a long time. Elephants have trunks which allow them to do just the same thing.

NEW EVIDENCE

Archaeologists often find new evidence about what the Greeks knew. But they do not always agree over what the evidence shows! If they only have a few parts of something, they cannot be sure what the whole thing does. Sometimes, even after working on such problems for years, they still cannot be sure.

Vase paintings show us everyday things that the Greeks did not bother to describe in books. This vase shows how they worked metal in a furnace.

archaeologists people who dig up and study things left behind from past times

citizens men who are born in a city to parents who were citizens. A citizen had rights in their own city that they would not have in another one.

city state a city and the land it controls around it

colony a settlement set up in one country by people from another country

democracy running the country by letting the citizens make the decisions

fountains places where water is poured out through a pipe

geometry is the part of maths which is about shapes and their movements

herbal cures medicines and ointments made from plants and herbs

infection something which gets into wounds and makes the patient sick

latitude lines drawn across a map or globe to make it more accurate and easier to use

longitude lines drawn down a map or globe to make it more accurate and easier to use

officials people who work for the government or state, running the country or city

papyrus reeds that grow near water and the paper that is made by pounding their stalks

philosopher a person who thinks carefully about things and how they work

polluted dirty

priest a person who works in a temple, serving a
  god or goddess

religious ceremonies special times when people
  go to one place to pray to a god or goddess

scholars people who study and write books

slaves people who are treated by their owners as
  property. They can be bought and sold and are
  not free to leave.

tax a payment that you have to make to
  whoever is running the country

temple a place where gods and goddesses are
  worshipped

ANCIENT GREECE

DISCOVERIES, INVENTIONS & IDEAS

JANE SHUTER

Heinemann
LIBRARY

First published in Great Britain by Heinemann Library
Halley Court, Jordan Hill, Oxford OX2 8EJ
a division of Reed Educational and Professional Publishing Ltd.
Heinemann is a registered trademark of Reed Educational & Professional Publishing Limited.

OXFORD MELBOURNE AUCKLAND KUALA LUMPUR
SINGAPORE IBADAN NAIROBI KAMPALA JOHANNESBURG
GABORONE PORTSMOUTH NH CHICAGO

Designed by Celia Floyd
Illustrations by Jeff Edwards and Donald Harley
Printed in Hong Kong by Wing King Tong Co., Ltd.

03 02 01 00 99
10 9 8 7 6 5 4 3 2 1

ISBN 0 431 00507 9
This title is also available in a hardback library edition (ISBN 0 431 00504 4).

British Library Cataloguing in Publication Data

Shuter, Jane
    Greece : discoveries, inventions and ideas. - (Ancient world topic books)
    1 . Discoveries in science - Greece - History - Juvenile literature 2 . Greece - History - To 146 B. C. - Juvenile literature
    I . Title
    938

Acknowledgements
The Publishers would like to thank the following for permission to reproduce photographs:
American School of Classical Studies, Athens p15 (right); Ancient Art and Architecture Collection: pp17 (left), 25, 28, R Sheridan p23; Bildarchiv Preussischer Kulturbesitz pp27, 29; British Museum pp11, 15 (left), 18, 19; Fotograf Nationalmuseet: K Weiss p5; Chris Honeywell p24; Photo-RMN: Hervé Lewandowski p17 (right)
Cover photograph reproduced with permission of the British Museum

Every effort has been made to contact copyright holders of any material reproduced in this book. Any omissions will be rectified in subsequent printings if notice is given to the Publisher.

Any words appearing in the text in bold, **like this**, are explained in the Glossary.